Poetry is Dumb.

A Debasing of a Snobby Artform

Anant Sharma

BookLeaf
Publishing

India | USA | UK

Made with ❤ on the BookLeaf Publishing Platform
www.bookleafpub.in
www.bookleafpub.com

Dedication

To every bespectacled, coffee-loving cat-person plant-parent who snaps along to slam poetry in dingy, out-of-business but in-vogue cafes.

Acknowledgments

Indeed. Acknowledged.

Preface

When this idea came to me, I quickly brushed it off as a joke. Why would anyone write a collection of poems that are so irreverent and unpoetic that they deride the whole art form? What does it establish? A few giggles? A sense of mischief? An irreverent demystification of art that reclaims it from snooty divas who take themselves too seriously? Maybe. Maybe not. Maybe f*** yourself.

But just like that pesky kernel of popcorn stuck in the nether regions of your molar for over three weeks, the idea remained obstinately present despite attacks from several angles. Now it belongs in the real world, where readers like yourself will say, "why??" whenever they check it out. The answer is a resounding "42," btw, in case you didn't know.

So read on, O cautious young padawan, and fear not the lack of artistry that follows!

For what is art anyway, if not an examination of itself?

You're a Poet, and Everyone needs to know it

Write a word
make it two.

"parody"
"chin chin chu."

Switch up the rhyme,
squeeze a lime;
if they can do it,
so can you.

Imposter? I hardly know her!

Who's to say who you are?
Good rhymes can only take you so far.

Get a tattoo,
Dye your hair blue,
and sit in a cafe all day long.
Now you realize—
You know it's true!
You've been an artist all along.

So put down the pen and plan your pretense;
Imposter or not, on you it depends.

Who's the Idiot?

Me, with my benign delinquency
You, with your unamused persistence
Us, with the question between us
Who's the idiot?

Them, with their utmost confidence
You, with your pedantic hesitation
Me, with my talent for irreverence
Who's the idiot?

She, with her br ok en sentences,
Me, with my ins pir ed plagiarism,
You, with your knowledge of poets from the
Indian diaspora with Canadian passports and a
surprisingly high amount of success,
Who's the idiot?

Steal Like an Artist

I saw the best minds of my generation destroyed
by madness, starving, hysterical, naked.
The art of losing isn't hard to master.

Love's not Time's fool, though rosy lips and
cheeks
quoth the Raven "Nevermore."

Though wise men at their end know dark is
right,
You do not do, you do not do.

Where the mind is without fear and the head is
held high
I took the one less traveled by,

And THAT has made all the difference.

Writer's Block

Ugh.

Writer's Remorse

Hmmm… could have done better in the last one.

Buyer's Remorse

You: Ugh.

(A)I wrote this

This is a poem,
typed by code—
no real thoughts,
just "word" mode.

No big meaning,
no heart, no soul—
just a bunch of text
spat from a scroll.

And guess what?
It's still a rhyme.
Bad poem, sure—
but it's poem time!

I've got Nothing to say

I've got nothing to say,
and I say it out loud, at the top of my lungs
screaming! shouting! yelling! bellowing!
roaring! booming! barking! and howling!

Words come out of my mouth and straight to the
ground they fall
as if they had no purpose or point at all
but I marvel at them nonetheless
as if the entire world should be impressed
at the vomit I commit to paper
there is no better way to savor
its taste.

Maybe one day you'll look at this regurgitate
lovingly
as a child I had birthed
brought into existence
with nothing else but sheer resistance

Maybe I'll find my audience in the Soviet.

All Words are Made Up

All words are made up,
just like their meaning.
and just like in art,
all interpretation is feigning.

a whim and a fancy not long ago,
some bloke put a few acts up for show,
made up his own tongue, and people played
along
for who knew better
and "how could the bard be wrong?"

so gonnate your fear,
flast your doubts,
put pen to paper,
and weezle your heart out.

For who knows what any of this means,
my blue is my blue, but it could be your green.

Half Way There

Don't look back now,
for the starting line
isn't that far behind.

and ahead of you,
a long way to go
before the finish line.

and here you are, stuck in the middle
of nowhere.
though it might not seem mathematical,
trust me,
you're halfway there.

Baby Steps

The baby cries and whines,
bawls and crawls,
before it even stands.

It falls and stumbles,
its confidence fumbles,
and on its arse it lands.

It tries again,
for months on end,
even though it feels inept;

It pushes hard,
even before the start,
even before its first "Baby Steps."

When Kendrick Met Keats

Kendrick & Keats got into a fight,
was calling rap poetry right?

Both fought with rhymes,
each more sublime,
'til the other one was aghast.
One made a bar,
the other an ode,
but neither one could last.

But rap is meant to be easy, made for everyone,
Poetry was high art; how could it be silly fun!

Finally, they gave up and proudly concluded—
"To think either is hard, is quite deluded."

There is no Secret

"I'm missing something,
something all of them know.
Something they were told,
while I was out, having fun."

"A secret has been kept from me,
reserved only for the best,
something that makes magic,
that gets things done."

"why am I not happy?"
"why do I not have success?"
"why was I left alone?"
—asked every single one.

The secret is no secret,
it's only just you,
so suffer, persevere, and win
like all humans do.

If you fake it, you won't make it

There's only one true way,
to truly enjoy your existence.
You have to stand your ground,
and be You, in your truest true sense.

Yes, pretense works for most,
and even gets applause.
But mostly those who're cheering,
are the ones who're themselves lost.

In a world that's tired of lies,
people crave true connections,
so speak your truth and be yourself,
and live your true intentions.

Meta-morphosis

This began as tongue-in-cheek,
but now it feels… kinda real?
I wonder what changed,
and I wonder how you feel.

Is it for better or worse?
Has the poetry lost its purpose?
Was there ever any at all?
Has this book actually evolved?

Nah, that can't be it.
Poetry's still sh*t.

Do What You Hate

Love is overrated.
It withers, fades, and goes away.
Hate stays.

Hate grows.
Hate enables.
Hate empowers.

Love, on the other hand, can only make you
happy.

Rule of Dumb

When the orange cartoon gets elected,
we are under his dumb.

Intelligence is a liability,
under the rule of dumb.

Values are passé,
any price is fair to pay,
it matters not what you do, only what you say,
under the rule of dumb.

Let the world swing into chaos,
Let culture reduce to a crumb,
May greed save us all,
under the rule of dumb.

Easy as ABC

ABCD
EFG
HIJK
LMNOP

LMNOPQ
RST
UVW
XYZ

Rhyme schemes are easy,
as you can see.
Literally as easy
as ABC.

Read Between the Lines

Oh, the talent and work it takes!
Nobody knows
how hard it is!

Everyone is focused on
what they are doing.
And has sharp dedication to their goals.

Be serious now!
Just a little bit of fun
can lead to an eternity of doom!

Not everyone who starts,
goes a long way.
So sit down and wallow in your self-pity.

Read between the lines.

Is This It?

Can't you see I tried?
I don't even like it.
I just lied.

You could try too,
or maybe lie too,
"parody"
"chin chin chu."

So take it forth,
this knowledge brand new.
If they can do it, remember—
You can do it too.